I0446612

Sale Force One

The introduction to Sale Force One

SALE FORCE ONE

Table of Contents

<u>This book is dedicated to Ted, Thank you for seeing the salesman in me and opening my eyes to the world of sales that I love so much!</u>

Sale Force One

CHAPTER 1- THE INTRODUCTION TO SF1

Are you ready to bring your career in sales to the next level? Ready to get more customers, sell more products, and make more money than you ever could imagine? If not, then I suggest you dig the receipt for this book out of the trash and get your money back. SF1 is a program for those looking to transform from an average sales specialist to a true sales professional! If your comfortable just the way you are and have no desire to improve your career then put this book down, quit your job in sales and get you a job in a factory somewhere doing mind-numbing monotonous work for an hourly rate and forget about making the big bucks.

This book is for the go getters out there, the men and women ready to put in the work necessary to live a much higher quality of life. The savages out there who are never ok with 2nd place. Sales is a career that is quickly evolving with new technology being introduced all the time. Some argue that sales is a dying profession, With

SALES TRAINING GUIDE

the introduction of new technology like car vending machines and home delivery of practically anything imaginable. Luckily, you came across this book and are going to allow me to prove otherwise. Not only that but I'm going to show you how to embrace technology and use it as a tool to make more sales and expand your reach farther and farther away from your dealership. I have sold machines and vehicle to customers in over 15 different states and have never left my home state of Michigan! Sale Force One is here to help sales teams everywhere transform into the best possible version of themselves and earn more business than ever before. SF1 comes with a 100% guarantee that your sales team will close more deals while maintaining higher margins than your previous process. I've been a highly successful Sales professional and Sales Manager in multiple different sales fields including Powersports, Automobiles, Construction, and Parts & Accessories. I let my sales reputation and provable credentials speak for themselves as I continue to hold practically every sales record at every dealership I have ever worked for.

  In future chapters you are going to learn some of the highly effective basic sales techniques that will never change along with the new post pandemic adapted sales techniques. As long as sales has existed there has been certain techniques and processes that distinguish an expert sales pro from the average sales specialist. Most of these differences involve the understanding of a few aspects of basic human psychology. You will learn how to use today's technology to help you be a more effective

SALE FORCE ONE

sales professional reaching an unfathomable number of customers and potential customers. We're here to help your entire sales team whether they've been in sales for a day or 30 years we are going to make them significantly better at what they do and advance their career to the next level.

SF1 covers the entire process from the beginning including phone training, CRM management, your online reputation, reviews, boosting your google rating, leadership training, and much more. There is no question that Sale Force One is hands down the quickest and most effective way to improve your sales career today. The only question is, are you willing to accept the process and follow the outline handed to you in this book step by step? If you are willing to implement the process and adapt some new habits, then you are going to be extremely satisfied with the trajectory of your career in sales. No matter what you sell, or what your title is at your place of employment, you will certainly benefit from the SF1 process. Now let's get started with lesson one and get you on the path to success!

CHAPTER 2- THE F.O.R.C.E. PROCESS

- F- Familiarity
- O- Overcoming Price
- R- Rapport Building
- C- Creating Value
- E- Executing The Sale

First impressions are a big part of winning a customer over without much resistance. It's extremely hard to overcome a bad first impression so try not to make yourself look like a fool. The easiest way to avoid a bad first impression is to simply just be prepared. If you are not ready to greet the customer properly then don't do it. When approaching a customer just take your time, don't chase them down like a mad man looking like a hungry dog after a steak. I like to forget that I am even a Salesman when I approach customers and just simply try and make a new friend. Familiarity is the very first step in the F.O.R.C.E. Process and one of the most important. It's impossible to become friends with someone that you are not familiar with so keep that in mind for a while after you make your introduction. Until you get past the 4th step

SALE FORCE ONE

in the F.O.R.C.E. Process it is going to be extremely hard to close a deal. Think of it like a pyramid, If you started with the point of the pyramid at the bottom and worked your way up to the biggest diameter the structure would all come crashing down. That's the exact same thing that happens when you make a deal backwards and don't take the time to follow the process. You end up with either no deal at all or a deal with minimal profit margin and a customer that is acting like a dingbat, demanding all sorts of additional accessories or warranties otherwise they are going to "take their business elsewhere!"

Take your time, even if the customer comes in HOT asking for the price of this one, Then that one, Then the one over there. This is one thing that separates a sales employee from a Sales Professional. The ability to slow the customer down and make them realize that you are the expert, and yes this is how you make your living. But make them truly feel as if you have their best interest at heart.

Introduce yourself properly with a good firm handshake and make sure to catch their name and for God's sake don't forget it! For a true sales professional, the most important thing to accomplish is simple "Make a friend!" If you can get someone to like you then they will listen to you and if they will listen to you then you have significantly increased your chances of making a sale. Elite sales professionals are capable of finding common ground and be relatable to anyone that crosses their path. I don't care if you and the potential customer have polar opposite religious beliefs, or you speak English, and they speak Spanish. Figure it out, open up your google translate app on your phone and figure out a way to become this person's friend.

One thing that is extremely important in sales is having the ability to leave the bullshit at the door. Energy is absolutely contagious and rubs off on anyone you come in contact with. Both good and bad energy, you can't be an Elite Sales Professional when you're constantly texting your crazy girlfriend while you are at work because she has trust issues. Leave that stuff at the door and you're going to instantly begin seeing a difference in your day-to-day performance. Trust me, I've been there and done that. I began stopping at the door and getting rid of any bad energy and bad juju. Actually, physically stopping at the door every day before I go into work, taking a deep breath, clearing my mind of any negativity or stress and go into straight SALE FORCE ONE beast mode. Remember, the sales process is SO much easier when you have a customer who is having fun. SMILE, smiles are contagious just like good vibes. If you smile, the customer will begin smiling 90% of the time and that is going to be the beginning of your friendship. One thing that I am going to return to over and over in this book is basic human psychology because that is part of our job. We read people, get them excited, make them believe, and much more. A good sales professional could almost be considered a psychologist with the sort of things they will be capable of after some practice and a good sales process like Sale Force One. These techniques work for not just customers and potential customers but literally any human being on earth so use it to your advantage in

SALE FORCE ONE

life. Improve your relationships with your co-workers and friends. Shoot, use it to improve your relationship with your spouse or significant other. Good vibes go along way and can bring your life in a direction you never thought possible.

I once got into an argument with the mother of my son on the way to work on a Saturday morning. It was so bad she started throwing punches at me and trying to slam my head into the passenger window, so I jumped out of the moving vehicle and walked the last mile and a half to work. When I got to the door I stopped, took a deep breath, and entered with my usual swag like I don't have a problem on this earth. That Saturday I broke the dealership record, Selling and delivering 7 machines in one day. Granted it was a busy Saturday and I had some probable appointments coming in but if I would have let my morning and my personal life walk through that door with me there is no way in a million years, I would be capable of a record setting performance. I had so many deals going on at the same time I had the owner of the multi-million-dollar dealership helping me make copies of I.D.'s and running credit apps. Moral to the story is if you begin portraying yourself as a true sales professional, you need to make sure you bring the same energy every single day you come into work.

I've been through some serious issues in my life but have managed to maintain my professionalism which is a big reason why I have never had a bad review and receive a ton of referrals and repeat customers. When you approach customers for the first time be certain to approach with your hand extended out ready to give them

SALES TRAINING GUIDE

a nice firm handshake. I prefer the phrase "Welcome to ABC dealership. My name is Matt, and you are?" Maintain a smile and a vibe that you would expect to see on someone that just won the lottery. Of course, MOST customers are going to let you know that they are "Just looking" but don't let that change your energy. That is to be expected in sales and its our job as sales professionals to overcome objections. Keep your smile and quickly reply "Heck yeah, what is it we are looking at today?" See this is where your good vibes are going to come in clutch. Nobody wants to be in the presence of a person that looks like they are there only because they must be there. No matter what I am selling I make sure to do my homework and know my products. That being said, this is not the time for product knowledge. So DO NOT get into a bunch of detail about a bunch of different vehicles or machines, whatever you are selling. Remember if you follow the F.O.R.C.E. process you will have a much higher chance of closing the deal and you will definitely make a better profit margin.

After you get the customer to be ok with you accompanying them as they are "Just looking" you need to now begin the familiarity process. This is a pretty simple process. For the first 10 minutes or so ask questions ANY questions, they don't even have to relate to the customers desired product. Ask them where they are from, what they do for a living, What products or vehicles they have owned in the past. Just get familiar with your customer. Be a good listener! If you can remember simple details about your customer, it will get you a much better shot at closing the sale when the time comes. So far you have introduced yourself and set a good first impression. Next is going to be Overcoming price, which is not always the case while making a sale, but most customers are going to want to know the price on this machine or that machine. This is a touchy subject, and every customer is different, but you are going to handle price questions the same. Get them to forget about it! Or at least try your hardest to avoid price until the time is right. To accomplish this, it is best to downplay price as a priority as much as possible and attempt to get the customer focused on the product itself. Keep your good vibes and a smile as you acknowledge the customer's question. A good example of this interaction would be.

CUSTOMER- "What's the price of the black one over there?"

YOU- "That one's somewhere around $12,000 I believe, I'm not 100% positive on that though I will have to check with my manager to be certain."

Then you will want to follow that up with something like this to get them to stop asking you every price on the lot.

YOU- "The price is the easy part! We all get them for the same price, I want to make sure you get on the perfect machine. Once we find the one, I will talk to my manager and get you the exact price and go over all your purchase options!"

At that point, most customers are going to allow you to continue with your process because you are beginning to establish dominance and take the sale into your control.

SALES TRAINING GUIDE

The next step in the F.O.R.C.E. process is going to be rapport building. This is the most important step in the sales process, If you take your time and build rapport with your customer correctly everything else will fall into place with less effort and with less negotiation. People love talking about themselves. So let them talk! Your job has not changed, you are "Making a friend" keep asking open-ended questions and get to know as much as you can about them and more importantly, don't forget the information you learn. The more that you can remember about the customer, The more it appears as if you genuinely care about them finding the perfect purchase. Always ask the five W's while doing your investigation process "when, where, why, what, and who.". Open ended questions are always going to get the most information out of your customer. When the customer leaves the dealership after the sale you should be able to input the customers Name, Location, Job, how many children they have, if they are married or not, and anything else you can manage to extract from them in the Rapport building process. ALL this information should be immediately added to your CRM not forgetting any detail.

After you build some rapport and get the information you need to get your customer the perfect purchase its time to find the product you are going to sell them and execute the 4th step in the F.O.R.C.E. process "Creating value". The more information you have at this point the easier creating value is going to be. Use their own words to sell the product for you. For example- If the customer stated that they would like to have a vehicle that is bigger than

SALE FORCE ONE

their current Honda Civic. They would like a SUV or a hatchback with less than 100k miles and newer than 2015 because they UBER for extra cash on the weekends.

They just told you the exact vehicle that they are going to be unable to say no to. If you have something on the lot that fits those criteria, then you should have no problem closing the deal. Let's say you bring them to a 2017 Ford Escape with 68k miles on it. When you approach the vehicle, you say in your same good vibe attitude "I believe this would be a great option for you!" then go down the checklist "the vehicle has well under your desired milage, its new enough for you, and it certainly has more room than your Civic but at the same time is not too big. What do you think?" They are probably not going to fall for the first option you show them because it's always something, usually something like the wrong color or interior. "Eh…. I kind of wanted something either white or black, this red is just too much for me and I have been a Honda man most of my life."

That's why I never try to bring someone directly to the unit that I believe is going to be the perfect one. I show them something close but allow them to see something they aren't all the way in love with that way when you finally get to the ONE, it will be love at first sight.

So, you take them over to a 2015 white Honda Pilot with just under 95k miles on it. Seems how you know this one is the perfect vehicle for them. You can confidently feel as if this is the product that they are going to get the most use out of and be the happiest with long term. So, you need to take control of the deal again and with absolute certainty inform the customer that "THIS IS THE ONE!"

SALES TRAINING GUIDE

This is the last stage of the F.O.R.C.E. process, "Executing the sale" Just like everything else in the sales process, this step is going to be easier if you stuck to the process and got the necessary information you needed to perform your duties as an Elite Sales Professional. After you inform them that "This is the one" you will need to overcome any objections the customer may have. You will follow up any objections with just simply stating the facts. "You said that you wanted something that was wither white or black, you like the color, right?" They are going to respond yes to all your questions because you are asking questions you already know the answer to. After you cover all the bases and you get your customer saying Yes to every question, it's time to ask for the sale. I will go over deal closing much more in further chapters, giving you the knowledge, you need to overcome any objections a customer may have and close more deals than you ever thought possible. If you implement the F.O.R.C.E. process correctly and do a good job listening and retaining information about your customer, you will find great success in the world of sales and receive more repeat or referral customers than ever. The F.O.R.C.E. process is an effective way to remind yourself to stick to the process and don't jump ahead of yourself making the actual sale execution harder than it needs to be. I will be covering each step in the F.O.R.C.E. process more thoroughly later in the book and breaking down each step-in detail giving you more tips and covering more scenarios that you may find yourself in on any given day. The more you practice the process the better you will be

SALE FORCE ONE

at overcoming objections and knowing how to handle your customers in the most effective manner. Next, we are going to introduce you to a CRM. Otherwise known as a Computer Relations Management system. Please do not take this chapter lightly and if you are new to operating a CRM then you will get plenty of practice and information on how to use it correctly maximize your potential to earn either a new customer, repeat business, or a referral that you received and learn how to make the computer do the work of 10 guys and make you seem like you didn't forget a single detail about your customer and their family.

SALES TRAINING GUIDE

CHAPTER 3- CRM MANAGEMENT

In my opinion a good customer management System, otherwise known as Customer Relations Management or CRM for short is hands down the most important tools available to sales professionals. It is an absolute must have in today's sales environment. The benefit of a CRM is undeniable, statistics do not lie!

There is a ton of different companies that offer good CRM computer systems like Microsoft, IBM, Apple, Harley Davidson, snap on, and the list goes on and on. A lot of product manufacturers have a CRM computer program to help sales professionals sell their products. There are even programs like light speed that have multiple benefits like Inventory systems with a CRM as well. But there is one system that I found to be the most effective and easy to use. I have used it for most of my career at multiple different dealerships.

Victory Solution's easy to use platform and site navigation has continuously brought me to the next level. Victory Solutions is a CRM designed for powersports dealerships but can be an effective tool for practically any type of dealership selling anything. Victory Solutions is worth more to the sales team than any 4 sales professionals combined. After becoming fully trained and completely understanding how the system worked, I was able to almost double my productivity. The most important part of a CRM is correctly entering the information into the system. No matter how you ended up with the information whether it was a face-to-face encounter in the dealership or if it was simply just Sales lead generated by an online inquire Some sort, you need to always enter every single thing you know about the customer because you never know what information could be helpful in the future , I try to be as specific as possible to help me not only remember the customer as much as possible but be able to help them out the best I can. I'll go over one with you, so you have a reference to go by.

A customer comes into the dealership named Alex Smith. Alex is looking for a used truck but needs something extremely specific. He needs a Chevy Silverado because he just recently wrecked his and insurance is going to replace it at no cost to him except it must be between those years. Even though I do not currently have a Silverado in stock fitting the criteria I still treat Alex like any other customer. I stick to the process, I " Make friend ". At the end of his visit, I make sure to give Alex a business card and do not forget to get his contact information. I remember when I first got into Sales, I use to be so awkward when asking people for their information. If that is you, then you're going to have to overcome that shyness as soon as possible. There should never be a customer that you spend 10 minutes or more talking to that you don't at least try to get their contact information. Most customers will give you their information if you just ask for it! Closed mouths don't get fed. If you spend 20 min with a customer and let them walk out the

SALES TRAINING GUIDE

door without getting their information, The chance of you making a sale to that customer is very unlikely. If you do get their information and put it into the CRM correctly you will have more opportunities to complete a sale aside from the customers visit to the dealership.

Alright, now that Alex has left the shop, I enter all the information I have into the CRM. I schedule a follow up phone call into the system 3 days away. I enter Alex as a "Hot Lead" meaning, If I had the perfect product for Alex, he was ready to complete the purchase process. This is how the entry into the CRM should look and what information should be there.

CUSTOMER NAME: Alex Smith
PHONE NUMBER: 616-820-4789
INTERESTED IN: Only a 99-02 Chevy Silverado
FOLLOW UP: 8/27/23 at 1:30 p.m.
NOTES: Alex came in looking for a 99-02 Chevy Silverado because he recently got in a bad car wreck and totaled his 01 Chevy Silverado. Alex needs this specific vehicle because insurance is paying for it as a replacement for his wrecked truck. I tried switching him to something different, (No Silverado's in stock currently) Alex had a ton of aftermarket parts on his wrecked truck so he is certain he would like to stick with that model and year range. He is from Detroit and works at a foundry as a heavy equipment operator. He is a Boston Red Sox fan because his father was a fan his whole life.

Alright so now that we have him in the system we can continue to follow up and try to earn his business. You may be thinking "Why would I spend the time putting someone in the system that I don't even have a product for?" The answer is "Because you never know what the future may hold." Yeah, your chances of earning Alex's business are very slim at least on his next Silverado. Unless you end up getting one in on trade in the next few days then all you can do is congratulate him on his purchase and keep in contact with him. All you have to do is stay positively relevant, you never know when one of his family members or maybe co-workers might need a vehicle. If you put in the work and made Alex your friend even though he did not purchase from you then you probably have a good chance to earn the business.

I work every contact I have in my system the exact same. I work every entry in my CRM until they verbally tell me to please stop calling them. The best sales professionals are resilient and the most successful are always the ones who never give up and stay positively relevant in their customers mind.

Back to Alex, three days after meeting Alex, I gave him a follow up call after getting an alert on my CRM dashboard. Before I dial his number, I look over my notes really quick so I can accurately remember who Alex was and why I did not complete a sale the day he was in the dealership. I see that on the day of his visit I did not have the vehicle he was looking for. So, I check my inventory list to make sure we did not get one in. There were no new units fitting the description, but I decide to give him a call anyways to make sure nothing has changed. After talking to Alex for a minute he breaks the news that he has just purchased the vehicle he was looking for and no longer needed me. I congratulate Alex on his purchase and to help build some rapport with Alex, I get him talking about his new truck just trying to get as much information about him as I can so I can use it later to build an even better relationship with the customer.

When our conversation was over, I had some good information to add to the CRM. The note looked like this. NOTES- I called Alex and found out he already purchased the vehicle he was looking for. Alex got a 01 Silverado with a 5.3L V-8 in it and 98,000 Miles on it. Its red and Alex is going to deck it out with a ton of parts he salvaged from his old truck. Alex said he will be looking for a cheap car next year when his daughter starts driving, so I will make sure to stay in touch to see where it goes.

6 months later Alex pops up on my CRM as a scheduled phone call. Before calling Alex, I look at the notes. Because of my amazing notes I remember exactly who Alex is and I have some good conversation starters to get him talking. After talking to Alex for 10 minutes or so I add a new note to the CRM.
NOTES- Called Alex to check in on him. He is doing good and enjoying his new truck. He did have an issue with some suspension parts being bent from the crash in his original Silverado. But other than that, he is enjoying his purchase and just been busy at work putting in almost 80-hour weeks. He is still not ready to purchase his daughters first car, so I am going to keep in touch and check in with him about 90 days from now.

The key to earning the business of a customer like Alex is to just stay positively relevant. Be the first vehicle

SALE FORCE ONE

salesman that comes to mind when he thinks about purchasing a new vehicle. I can't even count how many times I have earned a customer's business by just following up with them every now and then and paying attention to the details. Sometimes the way to the sale is going to have to be the hard way and you are going to have to put in the work. These are always the most satisfying sales for me because by the time comes to close the deal, you will know this customer inside and out and it will be personal at that point.

Your CRM not only allows you to earn the business of the everyday customer, but also the potential customers like Alex. Without a CRM there is no way in a million years you would remember to call Alex in 6 months after meeting him and NOT getting the sale so you could try to earn his business buying his daughters first vehicle. You would never be able to remember what Alex did for a living, or even what kind of vehicle he owns if you did not have your CRM to use as a tool.

Some CRMs like Victory Solutions even have features like training sessions for sales professionals. Some have automatic messaging on customers birthdays or sales anniversaries, and customer surveys to ensure your customers are satisfied with their salesman rating them and giving them feedback on anything they could do better. Snap on offers a system called Mitchell shop key that has some really cool features on it and Snap on even offers small loans up to 10k for practically anything you could possibly need done to a vehicle.

I try to have about 25-30 events scheduled in the CRM for each day except for the weekends. An event could be

SALES TRAINING GUIDE

anything from a phone call to an email to an appointment. If you operate your CRM correctly you should have no problem having one or two appointments each weekday and a minimum of four or five appointments every Friday and Saturday. The longer you are a sales professional the bigger your CRM customer list will be and the easier it will be to stay busy.

CHAPTER 4- OVERCOMING PRICE

Throughout the next few chapters I will be covering the F.O.R.C.E. process in more detail giving you the tools you need to be the most effective sales professional. We will skip over the first step familiarity because it is self-explanatory, you are just trying to feel your customer out and determine what type of challenge you are up against. The second step in the process "Overcoming price" is a little more complicated and can vary depending on the customer you are up against.

Sometimes you are going to come across a customer that is just downright miserable or a customer that thinks they know it all and do not need your opinion or expertise. These are the customers that are going to give you a headache and force you to be on you're A game otherwise you're either not going to make the sale or you are not going to make any money. Whatever you do, just try your hardest to not let it get to you. Maintain your good vibes and happy go lucky attitude at all costs, the goal is to overcome a customer's bad attitude or down to business frame of mind and get them to loosen up a little. Accomplishing this will make your day and the sales process so much easier and more satisfying.

When you are giving product walk arounds to your customer it is inevitable that the customer is going to want to talk about price. The reason they are going to want to talk about price is because you should NOT have a price tag on anything. "That's right!" You should not have a price tag on ANYTHING you are selling. Of course, having a price tag on a unit that you are trying to get off the floor plan or maybe it has a rebate expiring soon is not a big issue because you can show a big discount that more than likely another dealership is not going to be able to beat. But having prices on your units especially brand-new units is going to do nothing for you but lose you money.

One thing you must realize as a sales professional is that customers have been trained to think "Price...Price…Price" they have learned these bad traits over the years from bad sales employees and dealerships tying to push products on customers without even knowing the customers needs and if the product is the right one for the customer. Customers have been trained to focus on price first so its your job as a Sales professional to change this way of thinking and get them focused on which product is going to be the best for them.

As the professional you need to be capable of taking control of the situation and the deal in a manner that is non-threatening and incognito. If you left the sales process up to the customer, they would get the price on every single unit in the dealership then make their decision based on which unit they believe is the best bargain. Contrary to what the customer may believe, them getting the best bargain is NOT what is best for them. Sure, it's a bonus if the unit that is going to work best for them ends up being a good deal or has a good rebate on

SALE FORCE ONE

it that is going to make the customer happy. But your job as a sales professional is to use your expertise to find them a product that they are going to get the most use out of and have the biggest smile on their face while they use it. If you stick to the SF1 sales process you are going to be able to have your cake and eat it to. You will begin seeing more and more of your customers with higher satisfaction ratings while you maintain a higher profit margin.

When I first began my journey as a salesman, I thought my management team was out of their mind. I couldn't believe that we didn't have prices on anything in the dealership. I argued and complained, saying that "surely we are losing customers left and right customers need to see the prices!" as a uneducated and green salesman my belief was that the way the dealership was operating was dumb and ineffective.

Man was I wrong, and I am not afraid to admit it. It took me a little while to comprehend the strategy and really, I didn't fully understand it for a long time. Sometimes I can be extremely hardheaded and think that my way is the best way. It wasn't until I had some serious sales training under my belt and had done some trial and error with a few different tactics that I was finally able to admit I was wrong.

The more sales you make, the easier it will get for you to overcome the initial questions on price. The less of an issue you make it the less of a deal it will be. It doesn't take a sales professional to start slashing the prices on everything just to move some inventory and get some sales. Anyone can do that! Someone that understands

SALES TRAINING GUIDE

sales from a deeper perspective, A true sales professional is someone that asks the correct questions and listens to their customers. If you can ask the right questions and listening to your customers, you will be capable of using the information you receive to find the perfect product that fits your customers needs and expectations to a T.

Following the F.O.R.C.E. process also encourages a sale that does not involve the need for the sales professional to lie or deceive your customer to make a sale or a higher profit margin. You won't have to do unsavory things to earn your customers business because you are going to make your customer fall in love with the product you are selling them which also means they are going to be willing to pay a little more for something they can't live without.

When I start a product walkaround and my customer asks, "What's the price of this one?" I keep it simple and respond "I'm not 100% positive but I will definitely check on it for you in a minute" then just keep it moving and keep doing your product walk around. Remember, you're trying to steer the customer away from focusing on price and more focused on the product. The bigger deal you make it the more the customer is going to be focused on it. Responding with something like "Price is the easy part; we are going to get you a great price lets just make sure we find the right unit first" then keep it rolling and either ask the customer a question or just continue your product walk around. Obviously, this is not going to be effective on every customer and to keep the customer from walking out the door you are going to have to start giving them something to satisfy them. In that case just try to be vague and don't give them exact number and try your hardest to avoid giving out "Out the door" prices on units the customer is not 100% committed to purchasing.

Having the ability to blow over any price questions without the customers getting irritated and walking out is a learned trait that is just going to take time to master. The more practice you get the better you will become at getting past price and focused on the important subjects that are going to allow you to create and hold much higher value in the customers mind. When I say give them a roundabout number what I mean is when a customer is asking "What's the price on this one?" you acknowledge their question and respond with a range that is somewhere in the vicinity like "I can check with my manager in a second but I believe that one comes in right around 12-15 thousand" this will hopefully give them enough of an idea to know if the unit is in their price range or not. If they look irritated and want more specific numbers, then you will go directly to MSRP numbers. Even if the unit has a rebate on it and you know it has a rebate on it this is not the time to start knocking prices down and cutting your profit margin already.

As a sales professional you are going to have certain go to one liners that are going to become second nature to coach the customer into going the direction you want them to go in. Never forget that you are the professional here not them! Don't let a customer come into your dealership and start running the show. Take the customers temperature as I like to say. Try everything in your power to save the price conversation until the right moment and that moment is going to be after the customer is completely in love with the product and agree with you that if figures are agreeable, they will take it home today.

Another thing to be aware of is how the customer reacts to your round about pricing and if you are even in the right ballpark as far as how much they are willing to spend. A good way to get a customer away from the actual price of the machine is to simply ask them what type of monthly payment they can afford. The customer is either going to let you know that they are planning on paying for the unit outright, or they are going to give you at least an idea of how much they are looking to spend monthly. For the most part if the customer is somewhat realistic and has some kind of credit established you should be able to find them something that is in that range. This is part of your familiarity process and is the type of information you need to be as professional as possible and get your customer on the right product. Bringing up payment options is obviously not what you want to do in the early stages of a sale but for some customers it is going to be necessary to overcome their pricing questions and objections. Only use the monthly payment technique as a tool to overcome a certain type of price customer.

Just to be clear so you are not getting the wrong idea, we are not avoiding price because we are ripping customers off or price gouging our customers. We are not charging people more than our products are worth. What we are doing is getting the absolute most profit out of each product while also ensuring our customer satisfaction is at its highest level.

A good sales professional can produce the happiest and most grateful customers while maintaining large profit margins. This is easily achievable by a sales professional that has taken their time and asked the right questions. Aside from that the sales professional must be well educated in the products that they sell so they can use the knowledge they gain from the investigative process to correctly match the customer with the product of their dreams.

People are willing to pay more for something that is more valuable to them. You as a sales professional are responsible for building that value in the product that you sell. The more sales you make, the more you will be able to find your groove and figure out your own ways to keep the sale in your control. You will be able to hold off on talking about price until its time to close the deal. Just keep your composure when the price questions first start rolling in. Navigate your way with whatever technique you believe will get you back focused on the unit and not the price of the unit. The price questions might scare the hell out of you as a up and coming sales professional but the more customers you handle and the more personalities you interact with the easier, they will be to overcome. Never forget "Price...AHH, PRICE IS THE EASY PART, LETS MAKE SURE TO GET YOU ON THE ONE YOU LOVE, THEN WE CAN TALK TO MY MANAGER AND GET YOU A GREAT PRICE!"

CHAPTER 5- BUILDING RAPPORT

Now that we have slowed the deal down a little, we can focus on building rapport with our customer which will really ensure that we are getting them on the correct product. If you have done your job correctly you will begin to see the customer trusting your opinion and allowing you to be the professional. This is what differentiates a average sales person from a sales professional. If you don't take your time to build rapport, then there is no way to know for certain if you are selling them the product that is going to make the customer the happiest and the product that you are going to be able to build the most value in.

The dictionary defines rapport as "A relation characterized by harmony" Which is exactly what you are trying to achieve. If you and your customer are on the same page and you can extract the correct information out of them then your sale will be harmonious and come like second nature. You will not have to fight for the sale or feel guilty because you are selling the customer something that you don't feel is going to be best for them. I go into every sale trying to build a relationship with my customer like I would if I was trying to build a lifelong friendship.

SALE FORCE ONE

The more rapport you build with your customer the more you will begin to humanize yourself and not come off as just another salesman trying to make some money. The rapport building process goes both ways as well. This is the time that your customer is going to get to know you as a person and not just another salesman. If you just sit there and fire off question after question at your customer, they are going to feel threatened or like they are being interrogated which is not going to end up good for you I promise.

One of the best ways of getting to know someone is by trying to find something in common with the customer. Try not to overthink this, you can find something in common with ANYONE that walks into those dealership doors. I've never had a customer that at the end of the deal I wasn't able to have something in common with. Sometimes you are going to have to seem a little more interested in something than you normally would be but that is just part of being an elite sales professional. Remember, Psychology is the best way of earning a customer's business and the most profitable. Anyone can slash prices and have big sales events, but It takes a real professional to be capable of turning any and every potential customer into a friend and getting customers to purchase from you just because you are you and your dealership is your dealership.

Your goal is to create relationships with these customers that will have them not only ready to buy from you and only you but also referring friends and family to buy from you as well. If you do a good job in the rapport building process and truly establish a friendship with your customer, they will begin helping you even when they don't realize they are helping you. You will begin picking up sales that you otherwise would have never even had a shot at. Your customer might be at a family Christmas party or birthday and overhear Aunt Julie saying that she is in the market for a new car and is about to go do some test drives this week. The customer that you have taken your time to get to know and built solid rapport with is going to tell Aunt Julie. "I actually have a friend that works at ABC dealership, and he will definitely take care of you. I will give him your number tomorrow and have him call you, ok?"

When you end up getting a customer like Aunt Julie you are going to be pleasantly surprised at how smooth the deal is going to go for you. Your rapport building is going to be easy because you already found something that you have in common. "Their relative" and she will be coming into the dealership with much less of a wall up and because of word of mouth she is automatically going to be more likely to listen to your opinion and trust you as a professional. Of course, with these types of customers they might come in thinking that because they have a connection, and their family member is your "Friend" that they are automatically going to get a good deal. Which is another reason why we don't put prices on the units. If we had the prices on everything on the lot, then when Aunt Julie comes in to see us, she is going to expect a discount from the sticker price on the unit. We can still show Aunt Julie a discount in some way shape or form on the deal worksheet that way she feels better but it doesn't always have to come off the sticker price. There are other ways to make the customer feel like they are getting a good deal which I will cover some methods later in the book.

Don't forget to stick to the process and do not let the fact that a customer like Aunt Julie is practically a guaranteed sale allow you to stray from your job as a sales professional. You should always stick to the 5 W's and make sure you don't skip some the rapport building process to move on with the sale just because you know she is going to buy from you. Still ask the who, what, where, when, and why and make sure to enter it into the CRM as if she was any other customer.

People love talking about themselves, so this process is not very difficult the only thing that is difficult is remembering all of it and properly recording it in your CRM when the deal is done. To help with this I sometimes will make a occasional trip back to my desk and jot down a few notes on a sticky pad so I don't forget. I don't leave my customer waiting for a long time but just long enough to write down some important facts like this. " Don smiths aunt Julie, Goes to Yellowstone twice a year, works at Muffin top bakery, grew up in Georgia, lives in Kalamazoo." That way I don't have to ask the same questions over again and I have some good information to add to the CRM for my follow up interactions.

The more you can remember about your customer at the time of your follow up, the more the customer is going to feel as if you genuinely care and value them as a friend. This builds value in both you as the sales professional and the dealership as a whole. If it ends up coming down to you and a salesman at another dealership but you remembered to ask how the customers latest trip to Yellowstone national forest went and if they are making down to Georgia during the holidays to see their family. There is no question you are going to come off as the more sincere sales professional or in our case "Friend".

The more you interact with customers and the more friendships you begin to cultivate the easier this process will get for you and the more sales you will begin to see at the end of the month. I know some people are going to be.... We'll just say "Unpleasant" but if you stick the process and take over the deal, guiding the customer into a friendship that ends in a business deal rather than just a simple business transaction you will begin to see a difference in all aspects of your sales career.

CHAPTER 6- CREATING VALUE

Back to creating value, the 4th step in the F.O.R.C.E. process. This is the step that is going to make it possible to obtain high profit margins and create a customer experience that is highly satisfying and like none they have ever seen. Customers these days are not used to dealing with a elite sales professional and sometimes we have to remind people why it is so much more satisfying to come into our dealership rather than just purchase something on the internet or price shop every dealership in the Midwest for the best out the door price.

What the term Creating Value means is to create as much capital in your sale as possible. I'm not referring to capital as in cold hard cash, what I am referring to is creating as much value in their purchase as possible. Not just the value of the product they are purchasing but value in yourself, the dealership, the service department, your financing partners. Just every aspect of the service you provide as a sales professional. When you build value in the dealership, your follow up process, your finance department, whatever you can use to add value to the sale. You are going to begin to realize that deals are beginning to come easier and easier. You are going to begin selling at M.S.R.P. more than you ever have in the past.

SALES TRAINING GUIDE

One thing I should also clear up so there is no misunderstanding. Just because creating value is the 4th step in the F.O.R.C.E. process, that doesn't mean you have to wait until you get there to start building value. Of course, you will have to wait until you get a unit picked out before you can begin building value in the product so until you get to this point you build value in everything and everyone around you including yourself.

Hopefully, you are blessed like me and have the privilege of working with a good service department, parts department, and finance team. If not, then maybe just keep that part to yourself and do your best not to overpromise or exaggerate your services outside your capabilities. For the most part, if you are at a decent sized dealership and they are doing good then you shouldn't have to worry about these things.

If a customer asks you "how is your service department here?" your response is going to always be something along the lines of "You must not be familiar with our dealership! We have the best service department here. Our service department has never let me down. They are factory certified and keep up on our inventory better than any service department I have ever worked with."

Find a good complementary phrase that you can use whenever someone asks about them. The same goes for the parts department and any other department that your customer could possibly interact with today or in the future. This is all building value for the deal. The goal is to make the customer genuinely believe that even if they paid more than they might have at another dealership they still ended up with a better deal.

"THE BEST DEAL ISNT ALWAYS NECESSARILY THE BEST PRICE!" This is important and a what you need to try and instill in your customers mind if they start trying to beat you up on price. Of course, this only works if you are a sales professional capable of convincing your customer that what you have to offer is worth more than the next guy down the line. Because one thing is for certain, customers always have the option to keep it moving and purchase from any old Tom, Dick, or Harry that has the same product you are trying to sell.

With time this will come as second nature and you will begin creating value in yourself, your dealership, and the products you sell without even realizing it. Every time you interact with a customer, words will begin to just roll off your tongue and into the customers ear canal like a fine wine being poured into a crystal wine glass. That way when you get a question like "What kind of rates are you guys offering right now?" you can quickly respond without hesitation with something like "Oh I wouldn't worry about that, of course we are going to have to run your credit to know for certain, but my financing team is the best there is. They are going to get you the best rate that your credit qualifies for!" Whatever you do, do not start quoting rates that you have seen other customers qualify for of get into the financing too deep other than maybe mentioning some of your lending partners. This is not the time for that at all, right now you are just trying to answer the customers questions without locking yourself into some sort of agreement or promise. If they start trying to dig too

SALES TRAINING GUIDE

deep and ask too many questions just play it off as if it is no big deal and you are not worried about it in the slightest. Get them focused back on the purchase and off the price or financing options until the time is right. I like to say stuff like "yeah…like I said my financing team is the best at what they do. I would not even worry about that part. We can handle everything right here; you don't even have to step foot in a bank and we have the same incentives as anyone else like no pre-payment or early termination fees. You will see, I know you will not be disappointed!"

Just like having good vibes when you talk to your customers you also need to exsert confidence in everything you talk about. If you seem legitimately confident in your products, your dealership and yourself then your customer is going to pick up on that and carry the same confidence as yourself and believe that paying a little more for their purchase is well worth it because they are dealing with the best sales team, at the best dealership, with the best service department and the best financing available.

One thing to be careful of is coming off too cocky though. I have made that mistake when things are going extremely well, and you feel like you are on top of the world because you have already made over 30 sales on the month or whatever the case may be. Trust me, the customer is not going to react well to you bragging about how many sales you have made this month or how you are better than this dealership or that one. I promise I'm not trying to confuse you here or tell you contradicting information. There is a clear difference between bragging and being professionally informative. You need your customers to believe that you are the best at what you do because you care and because you take the time to create a customer experience that is better than anything they have ever experienced.

Sales is a career that gets easier as time progresses IF you know how to build rapport and create value while you encourage a lifelong friendship with your customers. Creating value in yourself can be something as simple as just being polite and respectful. Anything you do or say that is going to help the customer like or trust you more is creating value.

Another thing you want to try your hardest to avoid is downgrading and trash talking other dealerships or sales professionals. This is something that will not help you and if anything will only drive customers away. Sure, if they mention how bad of an experience, they endured from another dealership then by all means agree with them and listen to what their problem is and make sure not to make the same mistakes as the person or business they are referring to but just stay away from outright downgrading someone else in order to make yourself look better. I promise you; the customer is not going to react well to negativity. The best thing to do is to keep the customer present with you and excited about the purchase they are trying to make. Even when I am selling cars or something that might not be the most exciting to me, I still try to keep the deal positive with nothing but excitement and happiness. You don't have to reiterate the fact that your dealership doesn't do the things that ABC dealership does or and you guys don't do slimeball things like ABC dealership. The more you try to make yourself look better by talking about how bad someone else is only makes you look worse and will make the customer question your legitimacy.

Taking the time to get your certifications is another good way to create value in yourself as well. I get my certification for any product that offers it. This is just another tool in your toolbox that you can use when you need a little help. This is especially effective in the powersports industry. Getting certified on a product only takes an hour or so and can be accomplished in your free time in between appointments or even on your day off. But once you have it, you have it and nobody can ever take it from you. Whenever a new product comes in, for instance a Polaris General 1000 in stock and it's the new model year. I will take the time and do my certification quick before I even have a chance to sell it. When you do this, you are creating value in yourself as a sales professional. You now know your product inside and out and know what that product does best, what it can not do, and what type of customer that product would work best for. Its not good enough just knowing your inventory. You need to KNOW your inventory. The same goes for used inventory. I have had to learn a machine that was almost 30 years old before just so If the customer had any questions, I could maintain my professionalism and answer any questions they may have. If you have to you might have to google it but at least you will know that the vehicle has a 2.3l 4-cylinder engine in it and was the motor trend car of the year because of its safety and gas milage. Simple stuff like that can be the difference between making a sale a sale and having a customer walk out the door on you.

While creating value is an important step in the sales process you also need to be careful not to go to far. Have you ever heard the term "less is more?" well, with specific information this can certainly be the case. Just like you want to avoid seeming too cocky and douche baggy, you also want to avoid giving the customer too much information. Every customer is different, so this is just one of those play it by ear situations but remember…just because you know something does not mean your customer needs to know it. Save your product knowledge that you learn from doing your certifications and training until a customer asks you for the information.

I have witnessed multiple sales professionals hit a wall because they began giving the customers too much information. Filling their head with engine displacements and gear ratios when they don't ask for the information creates this. "Oh, wow….this is a lot of information. You know what, I'm going to have to go home and think about this for a little while and I will get back to you." Which obviously is not what we are trying to accomplish. We want the customer to buy TODAY! So, the goal is to know the information about the products we sell but only use it when necessary. This will create a much more professional atmosphere and not intimidate our customers.

I create value in myself by just flat out being a good person. I become in expert in the products that I sell. I

SALES TRAINING GUIDE

listen to my customer and in a professional manner extract the information out of them to help align them with the product that I believe is going to do everything they need it to do and not a bunch of stuff they are never going to need. I always stay prepared and knowledgeable in the products we sell. I bring everyone and every department around me to a higher level by speaking it into existence. The more someone hears that they're the best at what they do and the more positive feedback someone receives the better they are going to be. Remember, the entire dealership will benefit from each other. If you make more sales, then the service department will certainly receive more service customers and those service departments are certainly going to need to get their parts from somewhere, so the parts department is going to receive more business as well. This is a team business; no top selling salesman ever has done it on his own. Even if someone doesn't like you for whatever reason because you have had some issues in the past or whatever. Just kill them with kindness and smiles, and to the customer, they are the best at what they do. Nobody in history has ever had a better chance of making a sale after they say something like "yeah, our dealership is great I'm going to take care of you for sure, BUT…. the service department has a bunch of idiots back their so take your car somewhere else if you want to get it worked on!"

One of my favorite ways to create value in myself is to use my reviews as co-signer or maybe let the customer check out my evidence manual which we are going to cover later on in the book but if you follow the program you will have no problem having stacks of 5 star reviews and a hefty evidence manual that you can show the customer to make them feel better about doing business with you and ease their mind a little bit. This of course would be one of the last efforts in creating value and should be saved for a customer that is looking at deal worksheets but just is teetering on the edge of walking out the door.

I pull up my reviews on google and throw my evidence manual down in front of them and say something like "Listen Linda, I didn't make it this far in my career with this much good feedback by overcharging my customers or not taking care of them when they need something.....our dealership is always going to take care of you and I feel like we did an amazing job finding you exactly what you needed. Here's the pen, just sign on that line there and you can take it home today!"

You can never build too much value in your deal, but you can scare a deal away with too much information or by being too cocky and acting like a douche so find your perfect medium and start closing more deals at higher profit margins than ever before.

CHAPTER 7- EXECUTING THE SALE

Executing the sale is the final step in the F.O.R.C.E. process and consist of a few different steps. First, we must get a customer to agree that we have found the product that they are willing to take home today if figures are agreeable. In the next chapter I will go over the second part of executing the sale which is, going over a deal worksheet.

The better you have done your job and stuck to the F.O.R.C.E. process the easier this is going to be for you. At this point you should have professionally and knowledgably narrowed the customers selection down to 2 if possible. You need two products that both accomplish the same thing but maybe one is a little more expensive or the newer model year. You should have the product that you are expecting to sell them then the second option should just be there in case they are trying to beat you up on price.

This is where you get the customer saying YES! I went over it a little bit earlier, but I will refresh on it really quick, so you remember. Every question you asked the customer in the rapport building process that you can use as ammo you would use now. I'm going to go over a deal that I actually had in the past and closed the customer at

SALE FORCE ONE

full M.S.R.P. by doing nothing more than sticking to the FS1 process and not giving up.

One day in mid-July a customer named John came into the dealership a little HOT! Johns first words to me were "I NEED YOUR BEST OUT THE DOOR PRICE ON A POLARIS RZR 1000XP…. UP THE ROAD POWERSPORTS SAYS I CAN GET THE ONE UP THERE FOR $23,000 OUT THE DOOR. IF YOU CAN'T BEAT THAT THEN I WILL JUST GO THERE!"

All I could do was smile at John and greet him like any other customer coming through the door. "ABSOLUTLY…. WELCOME TO ABC POWERSPORTS IM MATT, I WOULD BE GLAD TO HELP YOU OUT TODAY. WHAT IS IT YOU LIKE ABOUT THE RZR 1000XP?"

John stopped and was a little standoffish as he asked me to please just go check if I can do it or not for him because otherwise, he was going to just go to the other dealership.

"YEAH OF COURSE LET ME GO CHECK ON THAT FOR YOU." I respond as I reluctantly go to talk to my sales manager knowing that 100% without a doubt he was going to laugh in my face and tell me to send the guy on his way. So, as I got to my sales manager, I gave him a quick rundown of what I was dealing with. My manager confirmed we were not interested in making a $200 deal on a new machine. I figured screw it, I have nothing to lose, maybe this guy can be switched to something different to get him away from the OTD price.

When I approached John, he was looking at some helmets it the apparel section. Staying upbeat and with a

SALES TRAINING GUIDE

big smile I tell him "HEY JOHN GOOD NEWS, MY MANAGER IS GOING TO CHECK ON THAT FOR YOU RIGHT AFTER HE IS DONE WORKING ON THE OTHER DEAL HE HAS RIGHT NOW, SHOULDN'T BE TOO LONG MAYBE 10-15 MINUTES" He let out a slight sigh but turned and continued to look at our riding gear.

"SO.....WHO DO YOU RIDE WITH?" I ask as I shadow him through the apparel department. For the next 15 minutes or so John and I talked about the who, what, where, when, and why. Quickly I began to realize that the machine that John was interested in was not the best machine for him and I might have an opportunity to earn a new customer after all. Finally, John asks "Can you please check to see if your manager has that OTD price yet?"

I run over to my manager and ask him what I should do? We come up with a game plan to get him switched to a different unit, one with some margin, and more importantly one that is going to make the customer happy. Armed with a manager that is going along with the program and an idea that just might work I approach the customer with a test drive forum in my left hand and a pen in my right hand. I keep it simple "My manager will be with us in just a minute sorry he is waiting on a call from the bank on a big deal and can't miss it" "But, He did say I could take you for a spin in the Can-Am just so you know you are getting the unit you like the most."

John is starting to get a little irritated so I assure him that we can just go on a quick spin and when we get back my manager should be ready to go. Now remember, this deal was rushed with only about 20 minutes or so to get to know my customer. But as we approach the Can-Am Maverick trail 1000 I wasted no time cashing in some of my deal capital by making him aware that with this one he would no longer need to purchase a trailer because the trail version fits in the back of his truck. That was one thing that he was worried about was having to borrow his father in laws enclosed trailer anytime he wanted to go out riding. Next as I fired up the engine and gave it some gas, I let him hear the power. John said the main reason why he wanted to RZR1000 was because that's what his friends have, and he wants to make sure he can keep up with them. Before we took off, I made sure to mention how comfortable the seats are in the Can-Am, John agreed as we pulled out of the showroom and around back with John in the passenger seat. When we reached the test track, I unbuckled my seat belt and got out, walking over to John's door as I opened it. "What, don't you want to drive it?" I ask as I stand there and wait. John quickly unbuckles as he runs around to the driver's side to have some fun. "I didn't know I was going to be able to drive it!" I look at him and laugh as I keep the smile and good vibes going "Just don't kill me today John but let's have some fun!"

It didn't take long for John to have the hugest smile on his face as we took a few laps around the test track. If your dealership doesn't have a test track, then just let your customer spin around the parking lot or in a back field. Doesn't matter, just get them behind the wheel. "THE FEEL OF THE WHEEL SEALS THE DEAL!" That's about the truest statement I have ever heard. If your dealership does not have a test drive program, then they are missing out. Clearly this is a part of a sales professional's job description to have good judgement here. You don't want to count anyone out as a buyer, but you also don't want to get hosed. If you feel like they are sketchy or if they are driving like an asshole, then shut it down fast and take back control of the deal. Either you drive at that point or stop the test drive all together.

When we rolled to a stop, I knew I had to keep the excitement rolling so I let John take a few deep breaths before letting him know that the machine he came in here for is not the machine that he should even be considering. John told me the only reason he wanted a RZR 1000xp is because his friends have them, and he wanted to follow suite. But when I reminded John that his friends ride on the dunes and plains. He is talking about doing that with his friends every once in a while but also trail riding with his girlfriend up in the Manistee national forest. Which I waited to drop this one on him until now but "John....IN MY PROFESSIONAL OPINION THIS CAN AM WOULD MAKE YOU MUCH HAPPIER. DO YOU KNOW WHAT THE WIDTH LIMIT IS FOR THE MANISTEE NATIONAL FOREST?" He answers "NO, WHY?" I rest my hand on the maverick trail we just test drove and break it down for him.

"50 INCHES.....MEANING THIS MACHINE YOU CAN TAKE ON THE TRAILS, THE RZR 1000 IS 64 INCHES WIDE SO YOU WOULD NOT BE ABLE TO TRAIL RIDE WITH YOUR WOMAN IN THAT, ALSO WITH THIS YOU DO NOT NEED THE TRAILER SO THAT SAVES SOME

SALE FORCE ONE

HASSLE, ITS STILL 1000CC MACHINE SO IT WILL KEEP UP WITH YOUR FRIENDS IN THE RZR'S HONESTLY PROBABLY BEAT THEM....HA.. HA...HA SO WHAT DO YOU SAY? IF FIGURES ARE AGREEABLE, YOU'LL TAKE IT HOME TODAY?"

John looked at me, then at the Maverick and says "I AM SO GLAD I WALKED IN HERE! THEY DIDN'T ASK ME ANY OF THOSE QUESTIONS AT THE OTHER PLACE AND THEY WERE ABOUT TO HAVE ME SPEND OVER 20K ON A MACHINE THAT I COULDN'T EVEN TAKE TRAIL RIDING?.....YEAH MATT, SEE IF YOU CAN GET ME CLOSE TO THAT SAME OTD PRICE I HAD ON THE OTHER ONE AND IS LONG AS ITS NOT TOO FAR OFF THEN I WILL TAKE IT HOME TODAY"

Knowing that the Maverick was already quite a bit cheaper than the RZR I knew this was going to be easy. My manager reminded me that the Maverick had a $1000 rebate on it, so I asked him to print me off a deal worksheet at full M.S.R.P. then one showing the $1000 rebate. In the next chapter I will explain in detail the process for going over a deal worksheet, which is what my manager is making up for John.

While my manager works on the deal worksheet, I open my computer and make up a quick deal jacket cover for the front of the deal folder. Another benefit of getting a customer to go on a test drive, you will already have their basic information to make a good, informative, deal jacket cover. This just speeds up the process and is right there for your disposal if you need to type their information in something like a credit app or insurance. Here is an example of how simple this sheet of paper should look like. Remember, we are just stapling it to the front of the deal folder and please keep ass sensitive information in the inside of the deal folder. Only fill out the lines on the deal jacket, do not add anything or miss any of the information. This will begin to come as second nature because they are never going to change. As the sales manager or finance manager you need to make sure to enforce this as well as every other part of the process. It is a process for a reason because it works, and it is effective so don't go changing stuff.

SALE FORCE ONE

Sales- Matthew Oomen

Date of deal- July 14th 2023

DEAL JACKET COVER

CUSTOMERS NAME: JOHN REAPER

UNIT: 2023 CAN AM MAVERICK 1000 TRAIL
STOCK #: 780269
VIN #: 276383453Y258
MILEAGE: 2

TRADE IN: N/A
TRADE VIN #: N/A
TRADE MILEAGE: N/A
TRADE NADA VALUE: N/A

IS THIS A FINANCE DEAL Y/N? YES

2 COPIES OF IDENTIFICATION. YES
DEAL WORKSHEET: YES
TEST DRIVE FORUM: YES
UNIT INSPECTION SHEET: YES
CREDIT APPLICATION:
INSURANCE VERIFICATION:
TRADE IN FORUM:
GOOGLE REVIEW:
REFERAL: NO
COMMISION REPORT:

SALES TRAINING GUIDE

Even though a piece of paper stappled to the front of the customers folder does not seem like it should be that big of a deal please just get in the habit of following the SF1 sales process to a T that means every single step. I established this process through lots of trial and error, there is a reason for everything I do. One thing that is for certain, you will not need to have to stop and hold up the financing process or forget to get a google review. That piece of paper ensures that you have done your job correctly. That you have all the information you need to move forward with the deal. Notice how I have filled out all the information possible at the time I print off the deal jacket.

Now staple it to the front of your deal folder and add your deal worksheet, along with your everything else you have so far which is going to be 2 forms of identification. One of them needs to be a state issued driver's license or identification. The second form can be anything that has the customer's name on it like a credit or debit card or even an insurance card will work, just something saying the person in front of my is who they say they are. You would have gotten these before the test drive along with the test drive forum. Now you are going to grab you're deal folder and go back down to greet the customer. Smile on your face like you just heard great news, DON'T FORGET TO HAND BACK THEIR TWO FORMS OF IDENTIFICATION!

<u>CHAPTER 8- DEAL WORKSHEETS</u>

Try not to take forever getting back to your customer with the deal worksheet either. Time kills deals never forget that. Time is the reason why it is so crucial to stick to the process and sell things the exact same every single time. You should never have a deal that is missing something or that you had to scramble to get the numbers together or whatever the case. Saving time and most importantly only having to do something once is the goal. You need your customer to still have the test drive fresh in their memory when you sit them down to go over the numbers. Just to be clear, a deal worksheet or what my version of what a deal worksheet should look like is in no way a legal binding document and technically means absolutely nothing. At least to us it doesn't, in the customers mind, they have officially just completed the purchase when they sign on the line. Next, I will show you what a deal worksheet should look like and how to go over them effectively and precisely like a true sales professional.

SALES TRAINING GUIDE

DEAL WORKSHEET

UNIT- 2023 CAN AM MAVERICK TRAIL 1000 DPS
STOCK NUMBER- 780269

PRICE- $17,099
TAX- $1,025.94
SET UP- $1,150
FREIGHT- $630
DOC FEE- $200

TOTAL- $20,104.94

DOWN PAYMENT- $2000
REMAINING BALANCE- $18,104.94

FINANCING OPTIONS

60 MONTHS- $337-$347

48 MONTHS- $422-$433

36 MONTHS- $563-$578

SIGN HERE- -------------------------------------
DATE--------------

SALE FORCE ONE

Clearly these examples of a deal jacket and deal worksheet are purely to show you what information you need to have on them. You can take your time and build them with your dealership's logo on them or however you would like. If the information is the same and the order is the same then, be as creative as your heart desires when designing your dealerships forums. I will show you examples of a few other necessary forums later but for now, lets focus on using your deal worksheet to help improve your closing ratio and front-end profit margins.

Back to John and his Maverick purchase. When I sat down across from him with the deal worksheet and a smile from ear-to-ear John couldn't help but smile back asking me "What?" I didn't have anything exciting to say or have a reason for the smile, so I just leaned forward flipping the paper towards John allowing him to look over it with me as I point to the paper with the end of my pen. I try not to be too serious during this process but also you must stay professional. Walk them through it step by step. If they have any questions, you MUST be quick on your toes and have an answer or at least a good response to their question. If you happen to get caught off guard and a customer here and there stumps you on a question. Just learn from it, Get the answer to your customers question, and remember it. Its ok to be green when you first begin your journey as a sales professional. With time you will be able to answer shooting from the hip with practically any question or concern a customer may have.

SALES TRAINING GUIDE

Back to the deal with John, When I sat the paper in front of John facing him so he could read it and I was sitting across the table from him, so I was looking at it backwards I ALWAYS start at the very top and work my way to the bottom. You are working your way down to that signature, with swag and maybe some would say a slight finesse.

At this point I begin talking about the unit we are on as if the customer already owns it. This will usually get another smile out of the customer and lighten the mood a little bit. Something like this. If you can please look back at the deal worksheet on page 42 and just read back and forth so you see where I'm at and what the heck I'm talking about.

"ALRIGHT JOHN, GOT YOUR PAPERWORK HERE ON YOUR BRAND NEW 2023 CAN AM MAVERICK TRAIL 1000DPS. STARTING FROM THE TOP WE HAVE THE PRICE OF THE UNIT, $17099……. AFTER TAX AND STUFF, YOU ARE LOOKING AT $20104.94 OUT THE DOOR. WITH A DOWN PAYMENT OF $2000 THE ACTUAL AMOUNT YOU WOULD BE FINANCING WOULD BE $18,104.94. MY MANAGER AND I RAN SOME NUMBERS FOR YOU SO YOU HAVE A CLOSE IDEA AS TO WHAT THE MONTHLY PAYMENTS WOULD LOOK LIKE. AT 60 MONTHS YOU WOULD BE LOOKING AT AROUND $337-$347 A MONTH. AT 48 MONTHS YOU WOULD FALL IN THE $422-$433 RANGE AND AT 36 MONTHS YOUR PAYMENTS WOULD BE BETWEEN $563-$578. If you could just circle which payment option would work best for you then sign and date at the bottom there and you will be driving home with a brand-new side x side in the back of your pickup truck!"

I know your probably wondering why I write in caps when I am explaining certain interactions with customers. This is because WE ARE EXCITED! REMEMBER. Not loud and annoying excited but more along the lines of so happy and in a good mood that you might just piss off Karen today because you are just having too good of time.

Of course, John just had to throw a wrench in the gears and start asking questions. First, he wanted to know what the exact price difference was between the RZR 1000xp and the Maverick Trail. I quickly settled that by reminding John that the RZR 1000xp was not even in our thought process anymore because its simply just NOT the right machine for him. To help him get over this mental conundrum in his head I brought up the fact that I have a couple of Polaris RZR 1000XP's in stock and if that was the right machine for him then by all means I would sell him one. But we can both agree that THIS ONE RIGHT HERE! as I tap my pen on the paper between us "But I would say that you will be saving around $2000 when its all said and done." He raised his eyebrows and pinched his mouth shut while shaking his head up and down. "John, I'm the best at what I do because I truly care, and I legitimately love this stuff. I like to spend my weekends riding just like you. If you would have never met me or if I would have treated, you like those other guys did and tried just selling you whatever machine I could talk you into purchasing. You would be waiting on your father-in-law to bring his trailer to you so you could transport home your new $25,000 paper weight that you might be able to take out 4-5 times a year max. You are going to have a smile on your face every single weekend for as long as you own this machine! Your relationship with the misses is going to be better than ever and be able to spend so much more time together having fun! Did I mention that you don't have to ask your father-in-law for any more favors!"

John hesitated for a second then reached for my pen as he circled the 48-month financing option before signing and dating the bottom of the deal worksheet. With a big smile like I'm the one that was going home with a brand-new machine I congratulated John on his purchase while I gave him a nice firm handshake to "Seal the deal" Of course the deal is far from over at this point but at least we can take a deep breath and relax a little. It doesn't matter that my deal worksheet literally means nothing to anyone. It meant something to John, and in his mind that machine was already his!

For you sales managers out there that are creating the deal worksheets you're going to want to run the numbers at a higher-than-average percentage rate. I usually run them at 12% and 15% for powersports purchases and a little less than that for vehicle purchases because typically vehicle purchases come with less interest. This is going to avoid a miscommunication with the customer. If they ask, then tell them "We run the numbers at that rate just in case you have terrible credit. There is nothing I would hate more than to have to come down and explain to a customer that agreed on numbers that their payment is going to be higher than we told them. We won't be able to show you your exact payment amount until we pull credit and send it to the bank for approval." This is what I must explain to about half of my customers with higher-than-average credit.

The second reason I run deal worksheets at such a high interest rate is because 90% of the time if not more, the customer is going to end up with a cheaper payment and rate than we agreed on. This information is used by your financing specialist. This allows the financing specialist to have some room in the deal for back-end products or services.

It didn't take long after implementing this new technique to start seeing results in our month end numbers. Our service contracts almost doubled, gap coverage, aftermarket warranties, and even apparel sales went up a significant amount. The way I was able to accomplish those gains was by staying one step of the customer at every point of the deal. The customer has no clue that when they are signing the deal worksheet at the agreed numbers that they are also going to get gap coverage, wheel and tire protection, or whatever aftermarket products that they may want. So its easy for the financing specialist to pitch them a quick one two on the back end products the dealership offers and how they may be beneficial to the customer when they can offer it at no extra cost. Of course, if the customer would like to turn down any additional services or warranties then that is up to them, and they can stick with the payment that is lower than what they agreed on. If the customer got approved at

SALES TRAINING GUIDE

a better interest rate than the deal worksheet then they could however add the back-end products they desire and remain close to the payment options, I covered in the deal worksheet. This is just a way to maximize the dealerships earning potential and help the dealership out as a whole. Depending on the lending institution the customer gets an approval on you can also use this payment leeway to add in some accessories or maybe some riding gear. For my automotive professional's out there you can use this extra capital to add in some new wheels and tires or tinted windows. Does not really matter what it is for, if you can get the customer to agree to it and have the lender agree to add to the value of the loan then you have just earned the dealership capital on the front and the back end of the deal which is the entire point. WE ARE SUPPOSED TO MAKE PROFIT THAT IS WHAT SALES PROFESSIONALS DO. I promise that extra efforts to earn the most amount of profit from every deal will not go unnoticed. Yeah, you might not get a cut from a back-end deal. Yeah, you might not care if the customer gets a new pair of rims and tires on their ride, but it will get you some appreciation from the parts department and to operate at the highest level you are going to need everyone you can on your side. You never know when a customer might come in ready to buy……If you are able to replace a part or add in a roof rack, whatever the case may be. When you help your co-workers out and are making them more money than they should have no problem getting you a passenger seat at cost to make a deal happen or get you a roof rack installed during the last 15 minutes of the day.

SALE FORCE ONE

Carry yourself as a true professional and you will receive the treatment that a professional deserves. Treat people good and you will get treated good. Complement people on their work and they will have a reason to do a good job. These are all just examples of a sales professional that knows how to network and build a team around them even if the other people on the team have no clue or interest in being your team member. The psychology of sales involves much more than just your interaction with your customers. We need to be considered a friend to anyone and everyone we interact with not just our customers. If you stick to these habits, you will start seeing a difference in your paychecks without question. I can't even count how many times a service department member or accessories department member has literally brought me over a customer and handed me a sale on a platter. They all had the chance to pick any sales professional they wanted to take care of their customer, but they chose me for a reason. They chose me because I am their guy, and I became their guy by becoming their friend and helping them succeed in any way I could at their job.

When you start carrying yourself in this manner and bringing everyone around you to a higher level it will certainly show you a whole other level of your sales career. Level up your career and help encourage a happier, higher paying, family type environment at your place of business.

CHAPTER 9- PHONE TRAINING

Anyone can pick up the phone and have a conversation with another person. It takes hard work, some humility, and definitely some people skills to become a sales professional on the phone. When I began my journey in the sales field, I had no clue how difficult it was going to be to become proficient at customer interactions over the phone. It wasn't until my sales manager at the time replayed a few of my phone calls so the sales team and I could improve our phone interactions and achieve the end goal, Getting customers in the door!

A good sales team should work on phone training at least twice a week at least until every sales professional is well seasoned and proficient, achieving high conversion rates. Even then it is still beneficial to hear yourself through the customers ears. You never know what kind of weird habit or quirk you may be oblivious to. I once was plagued by saying the phrase "You know what I'm saying?" I was shocked when we listened to 3 of my phone calls in the Wednesday sales morning meeting and heard how ridiculous and unprofessional, I sounded. After I was aware of the issue, I was quickly able to correct myself and was happy to hear during the next Wednesday sales meeting that out of 3 calls I was able to avoid that awful habit all together and guess what? Every week for the following month I was able to increase my conversion rate and it continued to increase for a long time before I finally hit a plateau. It takes years of experience and good training to become a phone specialist capable of building lasting rapport and getting customers in the door that normally would not come to the dealership.

I would venture to say that roughly 30% of my total sales can be directly attributed to my ability to convert phone calls to appointments. Your number one goal for a phone call is to schedule an appointment. Some CRMs available today offer services like phone call recording along with their messaging and voicemail services. If you are not blessed with this type of service, then do whatever you have to in order to figure it out. If you have to you can make a few calls on your cell phone and record them with a free phone call recording app. Post covid sales is evolving quickly and with access to all of the technology available today, we are receiving help like never before. You are going to discover ways beyond what I cover in this book. With time you will discover the latest new program or device that is going to help you achieve more sales.

After you finally listen to a few of your recorded phone calls and have a better idea of what you need to improve you can do mock phone calls to practice. I chose my own father to perform mock phone calls on. He was so confused when I called during the middle of the workday and started asking him questions and trying to get him into the dealership to check some machines out. But it was much easier and relaxed talking to my dad on the phone than it was a complete stranger. Next, I called my friend Troy and had a conversation with him trying to get him into the dealership as well. After my calls I hit rewind and listened to how I sounded. Quickly I realized that there was a simple solution to the problem, I should just pretend like I am talking to a family member or someone that I have known for a long time.

I know that sounds crazy, but it works. It will help you to stay calm and relaxed on the phone, Not stressed or anxious like before when you were nervously interacting with a stranger. R-E-L-A-X.....Like Aaron Rodgers would say! The same good vibes I talked about during the face-to-face customer interaction are going to be necessary over the phone if not more. People DO NOT want to take time out of their day to talk to a stranger on the phone that is trying to sell them something. Especially if that person sounds like their puppy just died. Always remember that the harder you try to sell someone something the less likely they are going to buy from you. The easiest and conveniently the most effective way to earning a customer's business is to be real, be interesting, and make them smile. Its nearly impossible for a person, I don't care who it is to be upset or angry towards you when you have a smile on your face and sound like you just won the lottery. Of course, a customer is going to throw you a curveball every now and then and try to ruin your day by being a rood, negative, or degrading. Don't let this take up too much room in your brain. Just brush it off and move on to the next call.

SALE FORCE ONE

Before you EVER pick up a sales call or dial a customer's number you need to get in the habit of taking a few deep breaths, get your mind straight, and always have your phone call worksheet in front of you with a pen. Get rid of any possible distractions meaning put your phone on silent for a little while, and make sure you don't have anything important going on that you might be thinking of in the back of your mind. Same thing as when you walk into the dealership in the morning and clear your bad energy walking through the doors. You will end up hearing all sorts of negativity during the course of your phone calling career and with everyone you will learn something new and eventually you will be able to take control of every single conversation and turn even the worst of customers into a lifelong friend. Some are going to take more effort than others, some will be fun, some will be miserable, but no matter how it goes a true professional always remains constant a even keeled. One the next page is an example for you of what a phone call sheet should include. Again, if you decide that you would like to add your dealership logo or whatever you think might make it look better than by all means have at it. In my experience this format is going to yield the best results and the most information out of each interaction.

SALES TRAINING GUIDE

Phone call worksheet

Call date- December 27th, 2023

Customer name- Michael Barrett   Call duration- { _____ }
Appointment- Saturday at 1:30
Interested in- 2024 Polaris General 1000
Currently own- 2014 Polaris Ranger 1000

Location- Cedar Springs, Michigan
Work- Shift manager Applebee's
Family- Married with 2 children 5 and 13.
Hobbies- He says none just riding UTV's.
Motivation- Happy family
Fun- Bonfires at his cabin in Baldwin and concerts

Current vehicle loan- Current unit's note is clear with no leans.
How did they hear about us- Driving by
Is this a referral- No

NOTES

Michael and his wife plan on retiring in the next year or so and moving up to their cabin permanently. They currently own a Polaris Ranger 900XP but are interested in upgrading to the General because of the new Ride Command features and the various other upgraded features. Michael is a Bears fan and has won multiple corn hole tournaments recently. He claims we must be able to get him at least $6,000 on trade or he is not willing to make a purchase. They will be in Saturday to check out some options.

SALE FORCE ONE

After the call was completed and I have my appointment set I CAN NOT forget to enter everything into the computer immediately. This is just a good habit to get into because it keeps your desk area clean and creates a less stressful environment for you to thrive in.

Before long you will be handling the BEST OUT THE DOOR customers with ease and a smile on your face. You are going to develop some go to one liner's that you will use often, and you will eventually know what you should and should not say to one of these unpleasant customers. I know it can be frustrating as a sales professional to refrain from giving prices over the phone but at the end of the day that customer is probably not going to end up buying from you anyways. All they are going to do is get your OTD price then call the next dealership down the line and ask them if they can beat that price. Clearly, they will be able to beat your OTD price. The customer is going to take their number and call the next dealership in line and so on until there is literally no point in even selling the unit because it is a $200 deal. We must start slicking together and not give in to these customers.

The only thing you can do with this type of customer is try your hardest to get them into the dealership. Use your phone time wisely and build some good rapport with the customer really trying to get as much information as possible while earning a little trust. If your dealership offers test rides which you already know I am fully supportive of then offer the customer an appointment to come take some test rides. I let my customers know that we can test ride anything we have available because I truly want to ensure that they are making the purchase that is going to make them happiest. Sometimes this works but of course about half of these customers are just simply hard to break and will probably go make their purchase somewhere else that employs a lazy and poorly trained sales staff.

When you operate like this you maintain control of the deal and refuse to let the customer influence the way you perform your duties as a sales professional. Be honest with them and break it down for them like I just did for you. Most of the time they will understand when you explain to them that this is the way you provide for your family and your dealership is worth more than the next guy. Most of the time they will at least listen why you explain why you believe this and if you have a good pitch and stick to the process you will have a chance at earning their business. Compared to you giving them a number on a piece of paper and letting them walk out the door I would say that is the better option.

The objective of a phone call whether it is a phone up, follow up, or a lead is always going to be the same, make a friend, build some rapport, and get an appointment set. Some are going to be fun and a good time getting to know a new friend. Some are not going to be fun, and you will have to strategize and formulate a good tactic to get the customer in the door.

Text messaging could probably be considered part of the phone call situation. I try to save it as a last chance option if I have been trying to reach someone for a little while but have not got in touch with them. There are a few reasons that I try to steer clear from texting too much if possible. Mainly because its hard to read emotion through a text message. That opens the door for your message to get misconstrued or off putting. With a phone call your customer is going to be able to hear your excitement and feel the passion for what you do.

When asking for an appointment the most professional way to go about it and a way to ensure your customer takes your appointment serious, limiting no shows and setting the basis for your customer that your time is valuable. Here is an example.

"Alright Mr. Customer so it sounds like you are going to make it into the shop to see me then. What day would work best for you?" You allow them to answer then reply "Saturday…I can't wait, I have an 8:30 a 2:15 and a 4:50 left available which one works best for you?" After they answer finish the conversation with something along the line of "Alright Mr. Customer I will make sure and have a few options ready for you when you get here and if you would like you can fill out a credit app online ahead of time for a factor financing process but If not then we can always do one when you are in the shop. See you Saturday at 2:15 I can't wait to earn your business!" Its more professional to set appointments and give your customer the service and time they deserve. Also, the deal process is less stressful when you take the time to get 100% prepared and have all your ducks in a row. When your customer completes a credit app on the dealership website you will now have any information that you did not gather during your phone call. This is useful

SALES TRAINING GUIDE

for completing your deal jacket and even making sure your paperwork is as prepared as possible which will have a positive effect on the customer and help them feel like they are dealing with a professional.

SALE FORCE ONE

CHAPTER 10-
ONLINE PROFESSIONALISM

As a trained SF1 sales professional you must start thinking about your public image and cleaning up your online presence. Especially with the internet of today, a strong professional online presence is a game changer and will bring your career to the next level. If you want to be elite, then you need to start from this day out acting like you are elite. Sure, you may be faking it until you make it for a little while, but the goal is to eventually match your attitude with actual evidence that you are that person. Even when you are off work you should hold yourself to a higher standard and avoid anything that could lead to negativity. If you claim, you are a sales professional then post videos of you beer bonging Yager on the weekend like a frat boy it is going to make you so unprofessional.

Maintain your social media accounts with precision and try to add new content as often as possible. This is why I take a picture with every customer sell to and try my hardest to get a 5 star review out of them. I will be honest with you and pass on my secret tactic to achieve near 100% review achievement with nearly 100% of them being 5-star reviews. I came up with the idea to give each customer a $50 gift card for anything in the dealership if

SALES TRAINING GUIDE

they leave me a 5-star review and allow me to confirm it before they leave the dealership. When I came up with the plan the dealership, I was working for was compensating the sales team with $10 for each review posted on google by a customer. My management hoped onboard with my plan and provided me with the gift cards to see if my plan was effective. Before long I was averaging about an extra $200 each week just for reviews and my customers were happy to have a little spending cash on parts or accessories. Clearly if you are at a car dealership or some other type of sales job that does not have a apparel department or somewhere they can spend the gift card at then you will have to pick up amazon gift cards or somethi3ng. Doesn't matter, when customers feel like they are going to get something extra to simply type out a few sentences on google they are usually grateful. If you have stuck to the process and provided your best customer service, the customer should be more than happy to give you your due regardless. The gift card just ensures that you are 100% going to get your review and typically its going to be a 5-star review which is going to help your dealership raise their google rating. After I began implementing this process, I was able to increase my dealerships google rating by almost 1.5 stars in less than 6 months. Before long it was included into our sales process and added to our deal jacket cover to be checked off upon completion.

I know some dealerships might not agree with this practice but at the end of the day you are going to have to work hard, think outside the box, and do whatever you need to do in order to secure as much positive feedback online as possible. 90% of the time the only customer that is going to go out of their way to leave a review is a pissed off customer which can haunt you for years if you don't smother it with as many positive reviews as possible.

Customers today have been trained to rely on online reviews as a form of gauging the trustworthiness of a business and depend on them to help them avoid a bad customer experience. When you begin to receive positive reviews on a regular basis and your reputation starts to improve online you will undoubtably see the benefits at the end of the month when you see your commission report. Anything you can do to get your name and your dealership in front of the customers eyes is going to help.

I believe that the best type of advertising is discrete, subconscious grasping advertising. What I mean by that is an advertisement that people don't even realize is an advertisement. An example of this is when get a picture with every customer I sell to and post it on social media. You don't have to go overboard and write out a whole paragraph about the deals you have going on right now or any kind of salesman propaganda. What you want to do is get your picture taken standing in front of the customers new purchase. I usually get the picture taken with the customer and I shaking hands. That makes it self-explanatory to anyone who sees the post. In the description section I try to just keep it simple and say, "Congratulations to John on his purchase of a brand new 2023 Can Am Maverick Trail 1000."

SALES TRAINING GUIDE

When a post like this comes across someone's news feed or they see it on your profile its not going to come across as you are advertising. When you make a post with every deal you will stay positively relevant in the customer's mind. You never know when that person may need a new vehicle or maybe they have a family member that is looking. They are going to think to themselves "Oh yeah, I should call that sales guy I am friends with on social media!" It just helps to keep yourself and your dealership in the front of the consumer's mind. The goal is to always be the first-person people think about when they think about your dealership's products or services. As a sales manager I make sure to confirm every sale my sales team makes gets added to the sales members personal social media accounts as well as the dealerships social media accounts and the dealerships official website. I also make sure to add my customer as a friend on social media and send them the link to the post when I post it. Practically every single time I have done this my customer has shared the post to their page which expands the digital fingerprint making it visible to all their friends as well. Birds of a feather flock together! Meaning, there is a big chance that your customer is going to have friends that have their same interest and could be potential future customers.

Humans are weird sometimes and will gravitate towards things or away from things without even realizing what they are doing or why. The more you try to push something on someone the less likely they are going to buy from you. Customers react to the subtle kind of advertising much better than the pushy, overbearing type of advertising. Not saying an advertising campaign every once in awhile in good taste is not effective. Just saying that creating content for customers trying get them to the dealership for a sales event or special sale is usually only going to cultivate a deal with minimal profit margin or customers that are not happy. I try to avoid sales events or anything involving cheesy sales pitches because it is off putting and is better left to the dealerships that employ an undertrained and poorly managed sales team.

YouTube is another avenue you can explore as you try to figure out what works best for your dealership or the products you sell. I found that YouTube is highly effective for expanding your reach to regions or states that you otherwise would never even be discovered in. For powersports I would try to upload content whenever we would get something unique or a new model that is usually quite popular. What I would do is lean the machine inside and out, all the specs, down to the compression ratio. Practice your product walkaround with customers or someone on your sales team for a few days until you are comfortable and hit all your focus points without missing any or misinforming anyone. Once you feel like you are ready have someone video tape your product walkaround showing the product with all its features and benefits in detail.

Yeah, this may never earn you a sale or it may earn you 10 sales it just depends on a few things. Make sure to get all your information correct or viewers will eat you alive and spit you out in the comments section. I try to stay positive and upbeat exactly like how I do when a customer is in the showroom. Steal their heart by staying luminescent and alluring. The more videos you do the easier it gets and the more professional your videos are going to be. My sales team always practices product walkarounds during our Friday sales meetings. We cover one product each week and each take our turn doing a product walkaround one after the other. When you hear it done in a couple of different ways you might pick up something that can benefit you when you are doing your video or with a customer. I once sold a Can Am Renegade XMR1000R to a guy in Florida who watched my YouTube walkaround video and called the phone number to the dealership which I flash across the screen at the end of the video along with my name. I expected to possibly expand my reach a little, maybe northern Ohio or Illinois but was not expecting to sell something on the complete opposite side of the country. After that I began producing more and more videos trying to upload new content at least once a week. All of my videos have since been taken down by dealerships I no longer work for anymore, but that Renegade video actually had over 700k views before my previous employer took it down because of a non-compete dispute we were engaged in.

Please make sure to remember this chapter whenever you make your next addition to your online presence and realize that stuff that goes on the internet is ON the internet. You must ensure that you are posting correct information that is astatically pleasing as well. Just don't post it if there is anything in it that could question your professionalism. No swearing, no trash talk, no disinformation or lies. Make sure your lighting is correct and there is nothing in the background distracting your viewers from your message. If you shoot a video, then realize that there is a horrible glare from the sun and it's hard to see something then just trash it and try again. This isn't one of those things that you are required to do or something that you absolutely must get posted by the end of the day. This is a complementary addition to your reputation and online presence that may or may not pay off. I do YouTube videos on slow days and in my spare time same goes for any social media content. Your sales manager is not going to be ok with you being stuck to your device all day on Facebook or shooting the same walkaround video 30 times in a row until you get it right. But at the end of the day, this is your life and your career so if you want to get to the top and operate on an elite level then you are going to have to start taking charge and putting in the work!

Your online presence is essential to the advancement of your career more now than ever in history. Post covid has been a roller coaster ride for our occupation and customers are relying on online information and reviews more than any time in history. We are transitioning to a new chapter in our profession that is going to be better and more profitable than ever before. If you would have told a sales professional 30 years ago that your customer base was over 1200 strong, they would have laughed at you and probably called the looney bin. The reason we can achieve the high level of customer interactions we do today are because of technology. It's a tool that we must include in today's sales process and sales training because it's the way of the future.

If you hear of something new that sale professionals are doing or have an idea that you would like to try, then by all means try new things. Figure out which ways work best for you to help get more customers in the door. Even if you only get one sale after making 3 different attempts at online marketing you have done your job. Just be careful not to overdo it. Too much of a good thing is not a good thing. If your online presence starts interfering with your daily phone call quota or your preparation for deals, then you need to figure out a way to balance your time more wisely. Social media and the internet in general can be very addicting and can lead to you neglecting other essential aspects of your job. That being said, once you learn how to optimize your reach with the help of your online profiles you can have the opportunity to earn more business than ever.

Although it may be tempting, price and out the door numbers is not something that we are going to get into on the internet. Conduct yourself in the same manner as you would if a customer called into the dealership because the goal is going to be the exact same, get the customer into the dealership. Tools like video chatting with the customer and sending them pictures if they request them is convenient for customers and can earn you some brownie points as you begin to build rapport and get to know your customer.

To make things easier on my customers I keep a tablet at my desk that is logged onto the review section on the dealership's official google page. This makes it quick, easy, and less of a hassle for the customer to leave a review. Don't forget to ask the customer to please mention your name in the review so it helps you specifically and not just the dealership. Some customers will just pull it up on their phone really quick and leave A review because their phone is already signed into their google account. But I would say 50% of all my customers if not more all have I-Phone so having the tablet available is essential. Especially if you are unable to offer any type of incentive for reviews it is extremely helpful to have something like this in place increasing your chances of building a strong online presence. I have a specific time that I ask for the review in every deal. I wait until the customer has completed their deal worksheet and submitted a credit app. For me this is the best time and I see the best results because its usually a boring and sometimes a little stressful time for the customer because they are waiting on an approval for financing. Again, customers are probably not going to leave you a review unless you ask for one or give them some kind of incentive so don't be shy, closed mouths don't get fed. We all know how long it may take a lender to get back to us on an approval so anything you can do to keep the customer occupied will help with your customers satisfaction and your professional appearance. I will get back to that later in the book going deeper into some techniques and time burners you can add to your process to make your sales a better all-around customer experience.

CHAPTER 11- LEADERSHIP

As you continue to progress your career in sales its important to become a good leader. Being a leader is not only reserved for the job of the boss or management but can be demonstrated by anyone that is ready to take their career into their own hands. You don't have to be the boss to be a good leader. But you do have to be a good leader to be the boss, so it is something that you are going to have to pay attention to and work on in order to bring yourself to the next level. Sure, you may get hired for a management position somewhere but if you are not prepared to be a good leader and have some experience under your belt then you will probably be chewed up and spit out. This doesn't mean you should go into work and start bossing your co-workers around or telling your boss what to do but if you see an opening and there is an opportunity to take charge and earn some respect then take it.

A good leader can come in literally any shape, size, color, gender, or age, and anyone can learn how to be a good leader if they have the desire. Some people don't want to be in charge and would rather just get in where they fit in and be content with their duties, but not me. Since you are reading this book, learning and trying to improve your career I'm guessing that you are not ok being a follower your whole life.

There doesn't need to be a big task or accomplishment that needs to be completed to start being a good leader. Simple things like showing up to work on time, being 10 minutes early to the morning meeting to hook up the projector, or just showing up to work excited to be there and spreading good vibes and attitude are all attributes of a good leader. A good leader should ALWAYS stay busy and never get caught sitting on the loading dock out back talking to chicks on a dating app or walking past a customer that has not been helped without offering assistance. A good leader always completes all their days task in the CRM like follow up calls and sales anniversaries and ACTUALLY makes the calls instead of just entering it into the CRM to keep their sales manager happy.

Having multiple leaders on a sales team isn't a bad thing. As a sales manager I hunt out natural leaders and try to add them to my team. When you have multiple leaders in the same work place it encourages advancement.

Its ok to ask questions and learn from those who are more experienced than you but make sure to pay attention. Sponge up any knowledge you can because if you want to someday lead others you are going to have to have knowledge on whatever it is you are doing.

If you have something to say, then say it and if you have an idea then let it be known. You need to start taking control and making it known that you want to be a leader no matter how small the task may be. I remember when I first started uploading YouTube videos online. At first my sales manager was not ok with me spending work time shooting videos and posting them online. One day he literally came outside while I was on my final take of a walkaround video and said to me "stop messing around and get in there to make some phone calls." So, I did what he said and wrapped up what I was doing before going inside to make some phone calls. On Monday morning when we got to the dealership there was 3 messages on the voicemail for me asking about the Can Am XMR1000R that I posted on YouTube. Within the first month there was over 20k views, and we received calls on it from all over the country. Long story short I was never hassled about "Wasting my time" with YouTube videos again and was given a little more leeway when I wanted to try out my next big idea.

Yeah sure, you can just stick to your dealerships process and not try to fix something that isn't broke but to be a true leader you are going to have to be imaginative and possibly even groundbreaking if you have a good idea. Like I was saying before a good leader should lead by example and look the part. Look down at what you are wearing, Dress for success. Start dressing like the person you want to become even if you are not there yet. Nothing says that you can't look like a million bucks when you are living in a trailer park and drive a 95 Honda prelude to work with no exhaust. Customers don't see that stuff all they see is you.

If you see someone struggling or need help with something that you know how to do, then step in and

SALE FORCE ONE

help. Even if the only way you can help is some words of encouragement ensuring them that they got this. If you are in a position of power like a sales manager or general manager this is especially important.

Be careful not to bite off more than you can chew. If you're not ready, then your best bet is to wait until the time is right. If you try to take charge and lead but lead someone right into a brick wall, then they are probably going to think twice about letting you take charge the next time.

If you are in a position of power and need to get a higher level of success from your employees a good way to get it done is to figure out a clever way to give them incentives. If you need to redevelop your pay scale to make some room for some sort of spiff bonus, then do that by all means. Its amazing what your sales team can pull off when they have extra cash up for grabs. You don't have to do spiffs every day but when you do have them, I guarantee that your sales numbers are going to increase. It just gives a little more excitement and competition for the sales team members and makes them push just a little harder to get that deal. You can give an extra $50 in cash or maybe gift card to each deal done on a Saturday or set sales spiffs of particular units you need gone. When you keep it separate from the employee's paychecks and pay up that day it helps with motivation because its something obtainable that day.

Another thing you can do is offer spiffs for the number of units they sell on a spiff day. So, if you decide this Saturday is going to be a spiff day then anyone who sells 2 units gets an extra $100 in cash, anyone who sells 3 or more gets an extra $200. However, you set it up the main goal is to create some motivation in your team and give them something to compete for. Stuff like this is never going to make things worse and will create a more fun and competitive work environment.

When you lead make sure to lead by example, lead with confidence, and lead people with integrity. If you are in a position of power, it doesn't mean you can't still get your hands dirty. Get in there and catch a sale every now and then and show your team how things should be done. Don't leave your team hanging if they are struggling and make sure to always have their back.

Setting goals for your sales team is a good way to keep your sales professionals motivated and on track to achieve their expectations. What I like to do is have my sales team all write down what they believe they can achieve for the new month. Usually, I will do this on the first sales meeting of the month. Every sales professional is going to be different based on their experience and customer base, but I encourage them to be aggressive and set a goal that is going to be hard to achieve. This gives them something to work towards and a gauge for the month to make sure they are staying on track. Every week at the sales meeting you can check to see where everyone is at with their sales and see if there is anything you can do to help them reach their desired goal.

In sales you never want to become complacent, in our career it is imperative to always keep grinding and never let up. When you have a goal set in mind at the beginning of the month you are going to keep grinding, keep making them calls, and give that extra effort in every sale to try and reach your goal. The best thing about setting monthly or even weekly goals is going to be the fact that you start from scratch each month. So, if you didn't have that great of a month previously, you will have an opportunity to redeem yourself and reach your new goal at the start of the new month.

It's important to also set some long-term goals as well. Long term goals are going to be your 6-month goals, your yearly goals, and even 5-year goals. For me I like to write them down on a piece of paper and tape it to something that I see every day like the bathroom mirror or on my computer at work. Somewhere that you will see it every day.

SALES TRAINING GUIDE

CLOSING STATEMENT

It's now your responsibility to do what you want with the information you have received. If you implement the F.O.R.C.E. process correctly you will start to see your career in sales reaching levels of success you have only ever dreamed of.

When you take your time with your customers and ask the right questions you will have a much better chance of earning their business and holding margin. Sale Force One encourages building strong rapport with your customers and creating a lifelong customer relationship.

Implementing Sale Force One and its process is NOT going to be the easy way out. It's going to be more work and more responsibility. But if you are willing to put in the extra effort and have the desire to bring your career to the next level it is the most effective way to do so.

Make sure to keep an eye out for other sales training guides from Sale Force One. Book two focuses on the marketing and advertising side of sales showing you more helpful tips on how to use technology to your advantage and expand your reach to customers you would have otherwise never knew existed. The third and final book of the series is going to dive deeper into the psychology of the sale and different techniques to get your customers listening to you and trusting you as the professional. As with anything you do, you are going to get back what you put in. If you stick to the process and treat your customers

SALE FORCE ONE

like they are family your customers are going to have a positive response. The process only works if you actually put the work in and prove that you and your dealership are worth more than the next guy. Good luck and congratulations on becoming a Sale Force One trained professional!

SALES TRAINING GUIDE